Editor
Gisela Lee, M.A.

Managing Editor
Karen Goldfluss, M.S. Ed.

Editor-in-Chief
Sharon Coan, M.S. Ed.

Illustrators
Ken Tunell
Kevin Barnes

Cover Artist
Barb Lorseyedi

Art Coordinator
Kevin Barnes

Art Director
CJae Froshay

Imaging
Ralph Olmedo, Jr.
Rosa C. See

Product Manager
Phil Garcia

Publisher
Mary D. Smith, M.S. Ed.

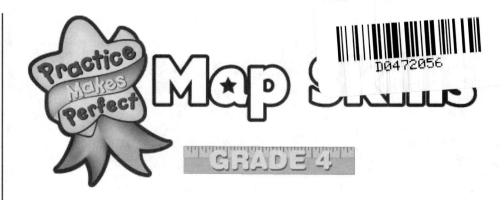

GRADE 4

Author

Jennifer Overend Prior, M. Ed.

Teacher Created
Resources

Teacher Created Resources, Inc.
6421 Industry Way
Westminster, CA 92683
www.teachercreated.com
ISBN 13: 978-0-7439-3729-0
©2003 Teacher Created Resources, Inc.
Reprinted, 2007
Made in U.S.A.

Table of Contents

Introduction

Using map skills is a great way for children to organize information around a fixed point of reference. The use of maps enables children to see and describe locations, landmarks, and geographic areas.

Using a map involves more than just identifying cardinal directions. This book focuses on the following map-related skills:

- reviewing cardinal and intermediate directions
- using a map key or legend
- measuring distance using a map scale
- determining distance using a mileage chart
- locating places and landmarks using a map grid
- understanding latitude and longitude

- identifying and labeling continents, oceans, and major mountain ranges
- interpreting a relief map
- interpreting a population map
- interpreting a product map
- interpreting a weather map

This book contains practice pages that are organized sequentially, so children can build their knowledge from more basic skills to higher-level map skills. Following the practice lessons are six practice tests. These provide children with multiple-choice test items to help prepare them for standardized tests administered in schools. As your child completes each test, he or she should fill in the correct bubbles on the answer sheet (page 45). To correct the test pages and the practice lessons in this book, use the answer key provided on pages 46–48.

How to Make the Most of This Book

Here are some useful ideas for optimizing the practice lessons in this book:

- Set aside a specific place in your home to work on the practice pages. Keep it neat and tidy with materials on hand.

- Set up a certain time of day to work on the practice pages. This will establish consistency. An alternative is to look for times in your day or week that are less hectic and more conducive to practicing skills.

- Keep all practice sessions with your child positive and constructive. If the mood becomes tense, or you and your child are frustrated, set the book aside and look for another time to practice with your child.

- Help with instructions if necessary. If your child is having difficulty understanding what to do or how to get started, work through the first question with him or her.

- Review the work your child has done. This serves as reinforcement and provides further practice.

- Allow your child to use whatever writing instruments he or she prefers. For example, colored pencils can add variety and pleasure to drill work.

- Pay attention to the areas in which your child has the most difficulty. Provide extra guidance and exercises in those areas. Allowing your child to color the maps in the book and/or maps of familiar places can help him or her to grasp difficult concepts more easily.

- Look for ways to make real-life applications to the skills being reinforced. Consider enlisting your child's help in planning a road trip or even a trip through town. The more meaningful the experience, the more likely it is that your child will learn and retain the skills.

Using Maps and Globes

You probably know that a map is a picture of a place. It shows where things are located. For example, a map of a bedroom might show where the bed, dresser, and closet are. A map of a city often shows streets, highways, schools, and attractions or landmarks.

There are many kinds of maps, such as world maps, country maps, state maps, and city maps. Weather maps can show high and low temperatures, current weather conditions, or even where people might be having problems with allergies. Product maps show the places where certain products are produced. For example, a product map might show that an area is known for raising crops, drilling oil, or raising cattle. There are even population maps that show how many people live in certain parts of the world.

A globe is a model of the Earth. It is like a map, but it is round. A globe gives a better picture of how the world looks. The round part of a globe rests on a stand and it can turn the way the Earth turns. Both maps and globes give lots of information about many kinds of places.

Answer the questions and complete the sentences.

1. A map is a picture of _____

   _____ .

2. What are three kinds of maps? _____

   _____

3. What are two things that might be found on a city map? _____

   _____

4. What can be found on a weather map? _____

   _____

5. What does a product map show? _____

   _____

6. What kind of information does a population map show? _____

   _____

7. How is a globe different from a map? _____

   _____

8. A globe is a model of _____

   _____

Compass Rose

A map uses a tool to show directions. This tool is called a compass rose. The compass rose can show the directions north, south, east, and west. Some compass roses show intermediate directions—northeast, northwest, southeast, and southwest. Some compass roses use full words for the directions. Some use the beginning letter to represent each direction.

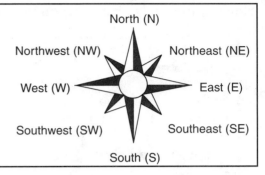

North (N)

Northwest (NW)   Northeast (NE)

West (W)   East (E)

Southwest (SW)   Southeast (SE)

South (S)

Write the direction word(s) or letters that are missing on the compass roses below.

1.
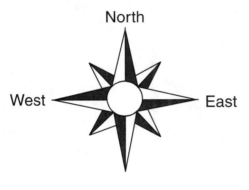

North

West   East

_____

2.
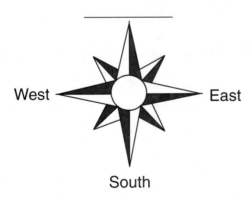

_____

West   East

South

3.
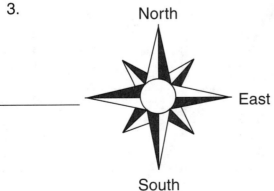

North

_____   East

South

4.
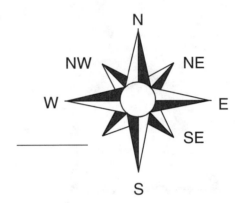

N

NW   NE

W   E

SE

_____

S

5.
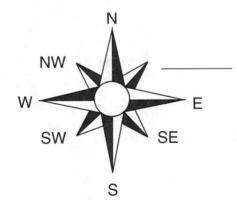

N

NW   _____

W   E

SW   SE

S

6.
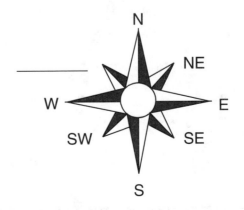

N

_____   NE

W   E

SW   SE

S

City Directions

Use the map to answer the questions on page 7.

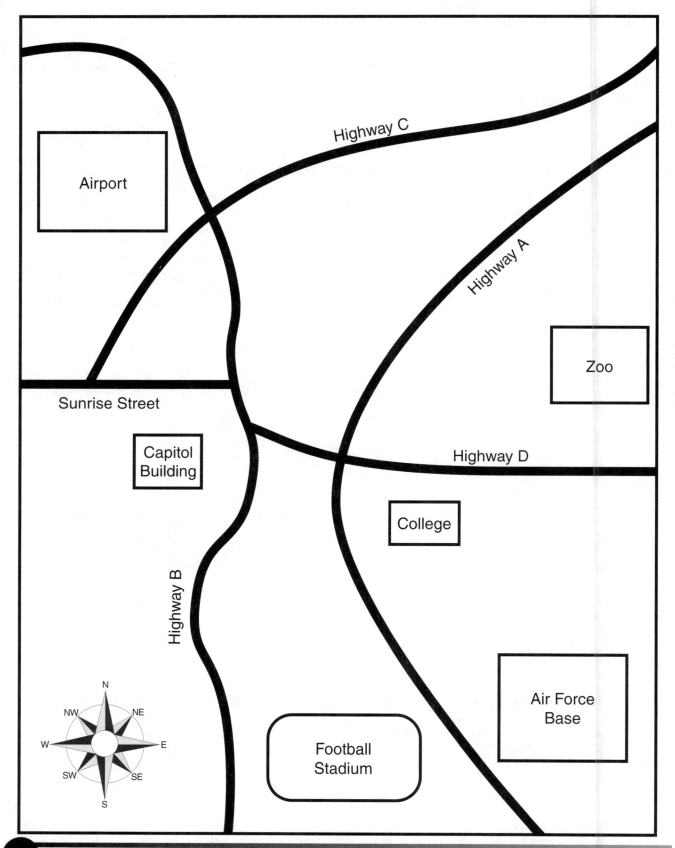

City Directions *(cont.)*

Use the map on page 6 to answer the questions.

1. Which highway is in the northern part of the map?

   _____

2. Which highway runs east and west?

   _____

3. What direction is the football stadium from the zoo? (Use intermediate directions.)

   _____

4. Does Highway C run northeast or northwest?

   _____

5. If you were at the airport, what direction would you travel to get to the Air Force Base? (Use intermediate directions.)

   _____

6. If you were at the football stadium, what highway would you take to get to the northeast part of the city?

   _____

7. What highway connects highways A and B?

   _____

8. Start at the capitol building. Travel north on Highway B. Then travel west on Sunrise Street. Travel northeast on Highway C. What is on the northwest side of the road?

   _____

9. The college is southwest of what location?

   _____

10. If you start at the southern part of the city and drive north on Highway B, what direction will the highway take you when you get to the northern part of the city?

    _____

Neighborhood Directions

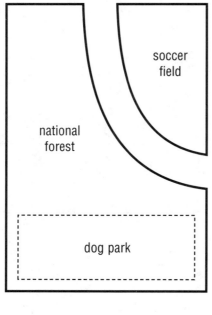

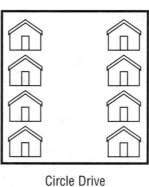

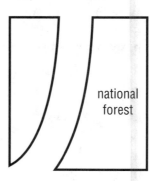

Circle Drive

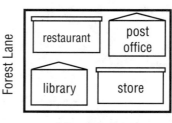

Forest Lane

Green Street

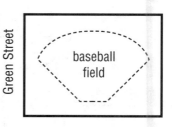

Mountain Road

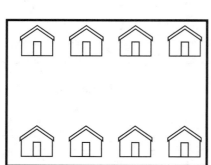

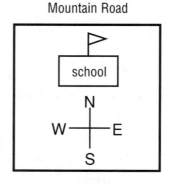

Use the map to answer the questions.

1. Which road is north of the school? _____

2. Which street is east of the post office? _____

3. Start at the swimming park. Go north on Green Street. Turn west on Circle Drive. Turn south on Forest Lane. What is on the west side of the road? _____

4. Start at the library. Go north on Forest Lane. Travel northwest on Circle Drive. What is on the east side of the road? _____

5. If you were at the restaurant and drove on Circle Drive and then Green Street to get to the store, what two directions would you drive?

   _____

6. Start at the neighborhood in the southwest part of the map. Travel east on Mountain Road. Then turn north on Green Street. Travel northeast on Circle Drive. What is on the east side of the road?_____

Map Keys

Maps use pictures or symbols that represent places or things. These symbols are found in the map's key. The key is also called a legend. Look at the two legends below. One uses pictures and symbols and one uses only symbols.

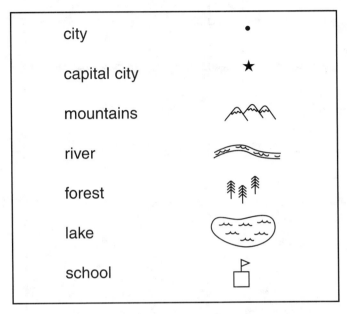

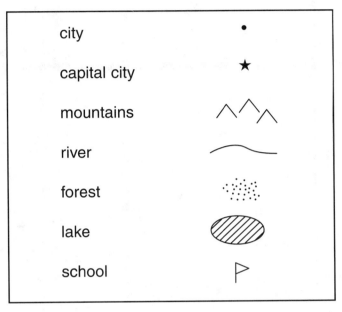

Decide whether each item below is a picture or a symbol. On each line, write picture or symbol.

1. • _____

2. ⌃⌃⌃ _____

3. ⋰⋱ _____

4. ～ _____

5. (ellipse) _____

6. ～～ _____

7. 🌲🌲🌲 _____

8. ★ _____

9. ⋀⋀⋀ _____

10. ⊳ _____

11. (flag) _____

12. (lake) _____

Map Keys (cont.)

Use the map below to answer the questions on page 11.

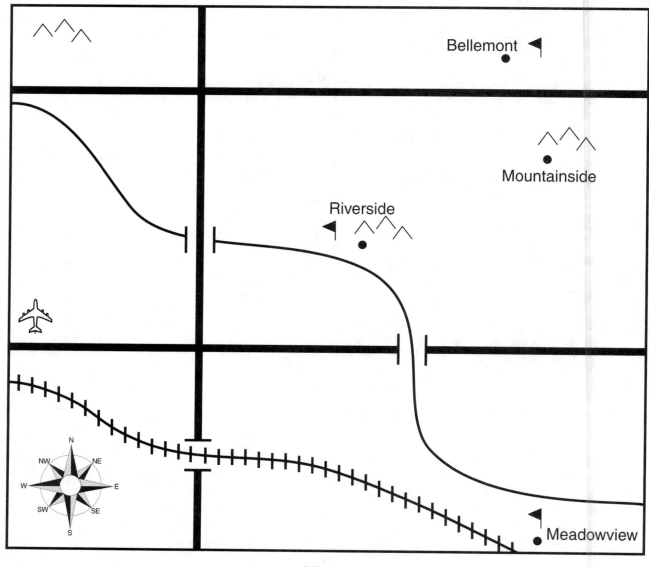

Key

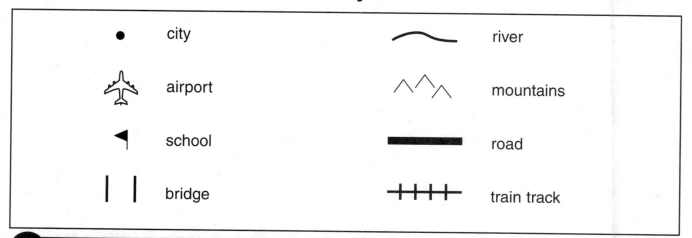

●	city	〜	river
✈	airport	⋀⋀⋀	mountains
◀	school	▬▬▬	road
| |	bridge	┼┼┼┼	train track

Map Keys *(cont.)*

Use the map on page 10 to answer the questions.

1. How many rivers are shown on this map?

   _____

2. Is the airport closer to the train track or the river?

   _____

3. Start at the mountains in the northwest part of the map. If you traveled along the river, what direction would you be heading? (Use intermediate directions.)

   _____

4. How many cities are shown on the map?

   _____

5. How many of the cities are located near mountains?

   _____

6. How many of the cities have schools in them?

   _____

7. If you were in Bellemont, which direction would you travel to get to the airport? (Use intermediate directions.)

   _____

8. Would it be easier to get to Meadowview by train or by airplane?

   _____

9. Start at Meadowview. Travel north across the river and one road. Then turn west. What city would you find there?

   _____

10. If you were at the airport and wanted to drive to Bellemont, how many bridges would you cross?

   _____

New York

Use the map to answer the questions.

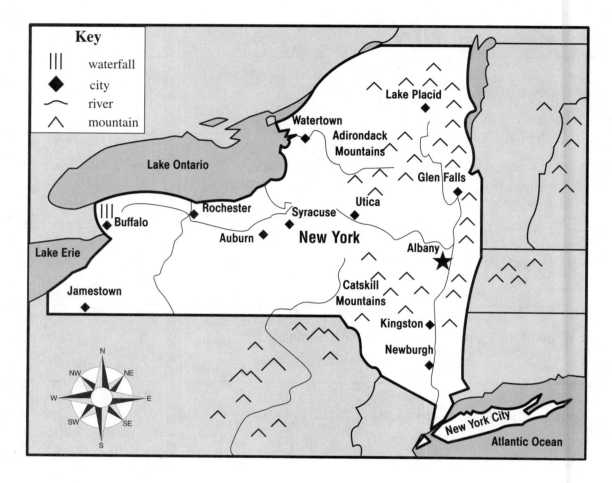

1. Which two cities on the map are in the Adirondack Mountains? _____

2. Which mountains are south of the Adirondacks? _____

3. Is Rochester closer to mountains or a river? _____

4. Which city is near a waterfall? _____

5. Which two Great Lakes border the state of New York? _____

6. What is the name of New York's capital city? _____

7. Is Albany closer to a waterfall or mountains? _____

8. Start in Watertown. Travel south past Syracuse. Turn east. Will you pass a river or mountains before reaching Albany? _____

Wales

Use the map and the legend to answer the questions.

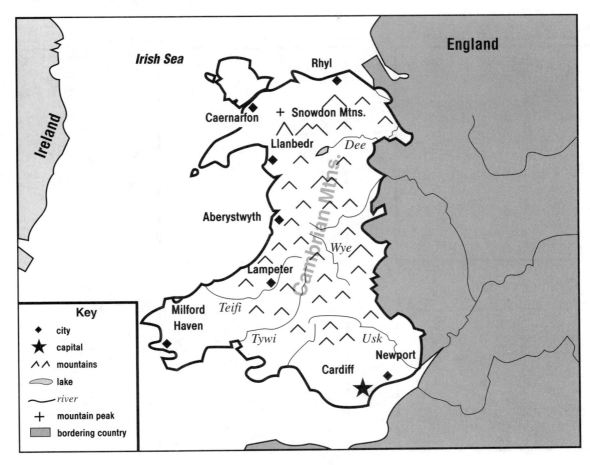

1. What country borders Wales? _____

2. What country is separated from Wales by a large body of water? _____

3. What is the name of the capital city? _____

4. A mountain peak is located in what part of Wales? (Use a cardinal direction.) _____

5. Is the lake in the northern or southern part of the country? _____

6. If you traveled from Newport to Milford Haven, would you cross a river or a mountain range?

   _____

7. Which mountain range is closest to Lampeter?_____

8. What river flows into the lake? _____

Create a Map

Use the directions on page 15 to draw a map below.

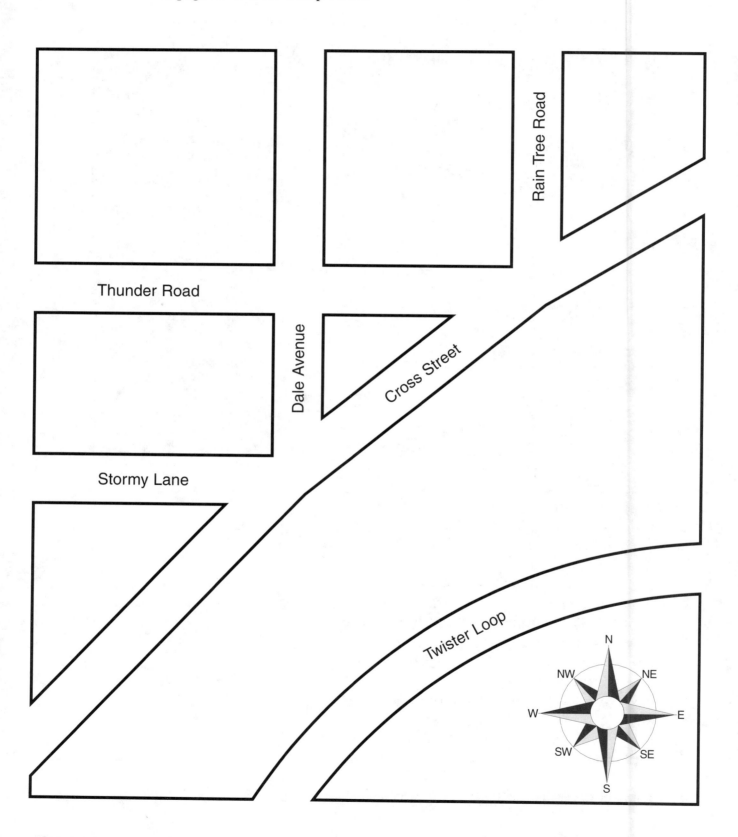

Rain Tree Road

Thunder Road

Dale Avenue

Cross Street

Stormy Lane

Twister Loop

Create a Map *(cont.)*

Use the directions and symbols below to complete the map on page 14.

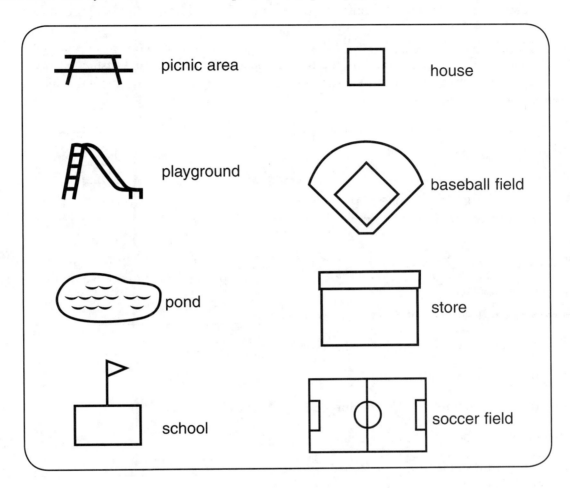

picnic area

house

playground

baseball field

pond

store

school

soccer field

1. Draw a pond in the southeast corner of the map.

2. Draw a picnic area northwest of Thunder Road and Dale Avenue.

3. Draw a baseball field south of where Rain Tree Road meets Cross Street.

4. Draw the school in the northeast corner of the map.

5. Draw a playground south of Stormy Lane.

6. Draw the soccer field in the southwest corner of the map.

7. Draw the ice cream store on the northeast corner where Stormy Lane meets Cross Street and Dale Avenue.

8. Draw four houses on each side of Stormy Lane and Twister Loop.

Using a Map Scale

Things on a map are drawn smaller than they actually are. A scale is a tool used to measure distance on a map. You can use a scale to figure out the number of miles or kilometers there are between locations.

Look at the two scales below. They each give a measurement on a map and what that means in terms of distance. On the first scale, one inch on a map equals one mile in actual distance. If two cities were two inches apart on a map, they would actually be two miles apart. On the second scale, one centimeter equals one kilometer in actual distance.

Scales

0 1
1 inch = 1 mile

0 1
1 cm = 1 km

Use the scales on this page to answer the questions about the map below. Use a ruler to help you. (*Hint:* If you do not have a ruler, draw the two scales on a piece of paper and use them to help you measure.)

1. How many miles does one inch equal on this map? _____

2. How many inches is it from Pine Shadows to Conifer Valley?_____

3. How many miles does that equal?_____

4. How many centimeters is it from Spruce Mountain to Ponderosa Hills?_____

5. How many kilometers does that equal?_____

6. How many miles is it from Ponderosa Hills to Conifer Valley?_____

7. How many kilometers is it from Ponderosa Hills to Pine Shadows?_____

8. How many miles is it from Spruce Mountain to Conifer Valley?_____

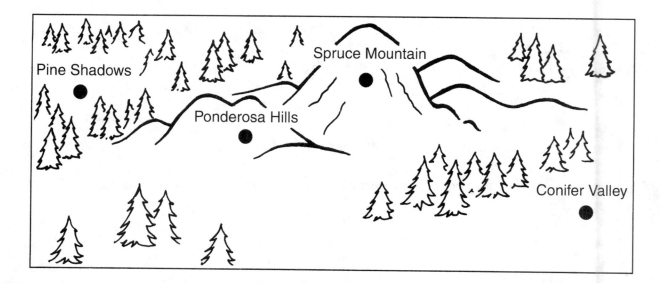

Map Scales and Distances

The map below uses a scale to measure distance between locations. You can see that one inch on the map equals 10 yards. Use the scale to answer the questions about the map. (You can use a ruler or trace the scale on a slip of paper to help.)

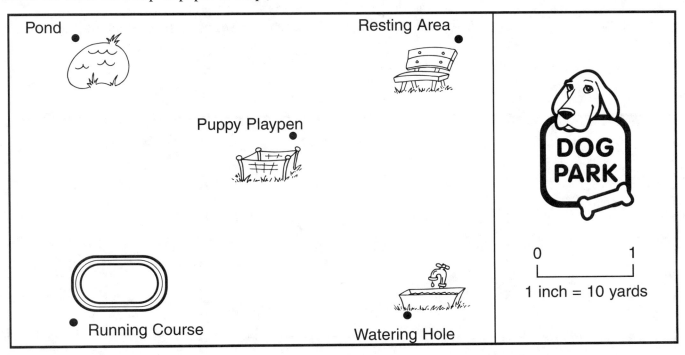

1. Measure the distance between the pond and the running course. You should measure 3 inches. How many yards does that equal?

   _____

2. Measure the distance between the resting area and the puppy playpen.

   How many inches did you measure? _____

   How many yards does that equal? _____

3. Measure the distance between the pond and the watering hole. You should measure 4 ½ inches. How many yards does that equal?

   _____

4. How many yards is it from the running course to the watering hole?

   _____

5. If you were at the puppy playpen, how many yards would you walk if you went to the running course and then to the watering hole?

   _____

6. If you were at the resting area, how many yards would you walk if you went to the pond and then to the watering hole?

   _____

Mexico City

Some map scales are not measured from inches to miles or from centimeters to kilometers. Some scales show a line that represents the distance on the map and then tell the number of miles (m) or kilometers (km). Look at the scale in the map below.

Trace the scale onto a slip of paper. Use the scale to answer the questions on page 19 about Mexico City.

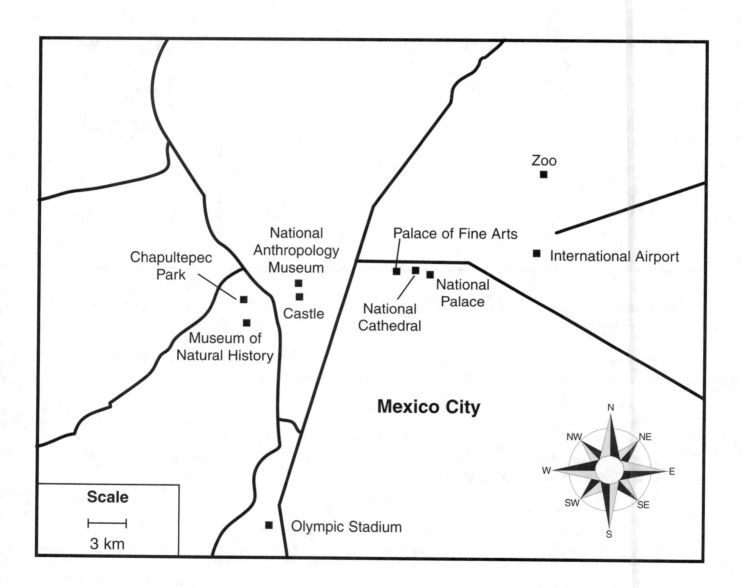

Mexico City *(cont.)*

Use the map and scale on page 18 to answer the questions below.

1. How many kilometers is it from the zoo to the airport? _____

2. How many kilometers is it from the Olympic Stadium to the National Palace? _____

3. Which is closer to the castle, the Olympic Stadium or the Palace of Fine Arts?

   _____

4. How far is it from the National Cathedral to the Museum of Natural History? _____

5. How far is it from the National Anthropology Museum to the National Cathedral? _____

6. Start at the Olympic Stadium. Then travel to the castle and then to the zoo. How many kilometers is it? _____

7. Is it farther to go from the airport to the zoo or from the history museum to the castle?

   _____

8. Start at the castle. Then travel to the airport and then to the Olympic Stadium. How many kilometers is it? _____

9. How many kilometers is it from the zoo to the west side of the park? _____

10. How many kilometers would you travel if you started at the cathedral, then went to the history museum and then went to the National Palace? _____

Mileage Charts

Sometimes maps include mileage charts. These tell how many miles (or kilometers) a person would drive from one place to another.

In the left column, find Denver, Colorado. Now, follow the row across until you reach Boston, MA. You can see that if you drove from Denver to Boston it would be 1,949 miles.

Use the mileage chart to answer the questions on page 21.

United States Mileage Chart

	Atlanta, GA	Boston, MA	Chicago, IL	Dallas, TX	Los Angeles, CA	Memphis, TN	Minneapolis, MN	New York, NY
Amarillo, TX	1,097	1,897	1,043	358	1,091	726	975	1,704
Denver, CO	1,398	1,949	996	781	1,059	1,040	920	1,771
Flagstaff, AZ	1,704	2,495	1,604	961	484	1,333	1,481	2,302
Miami, FL	655	1,504	1,329	1,300	2,687	997	1,723	1,308
New Orleans, LA	479	1,507	912	496	1,883	390	1,214	1,311
Norfolk, VA	540	558	831	1,329	2,694	877	1,236	362
Pittsburgh, PA	687	574	452	1,204	2,426	752	857	368
Tulsa, OK	772	1,537	683	257	1,452	401	695	1,344

Mileage Charts *(cont.)*

Use the mileage chart on page 20 to answer the questions below.

1. How many miles is it from Tulsa to Los Angeles? _____

2. How many miles is it from New Orleans to Boston? _____

3. Is Amarillo or Miami closer to Memphis? _____

4. Is Minneapolis or Dallas closer to Tulsa? _____

5. If you drove from Flagstaff to Dallas and then to Amarillo, how many miles would you drive?

   _____

6. If you drove from Miami to Chicago and then to Denver, how many miles would that be?

   _____

7. If a person drove about 50 miles per hour, how many hours would it take to get from Flagstaff to Memphis? _____

8. If a person drove about 50 miles per hour, how many hours would it take to get from Miami to New York and then to Norfolk?_____

9. If you were in New Orleans, would it take longer to get to Chicago or Atlanta? _____

10. If you were in Pittsburgh, would it take longer to get to Minneapolis or Atlanta? _____

Using a Grid

    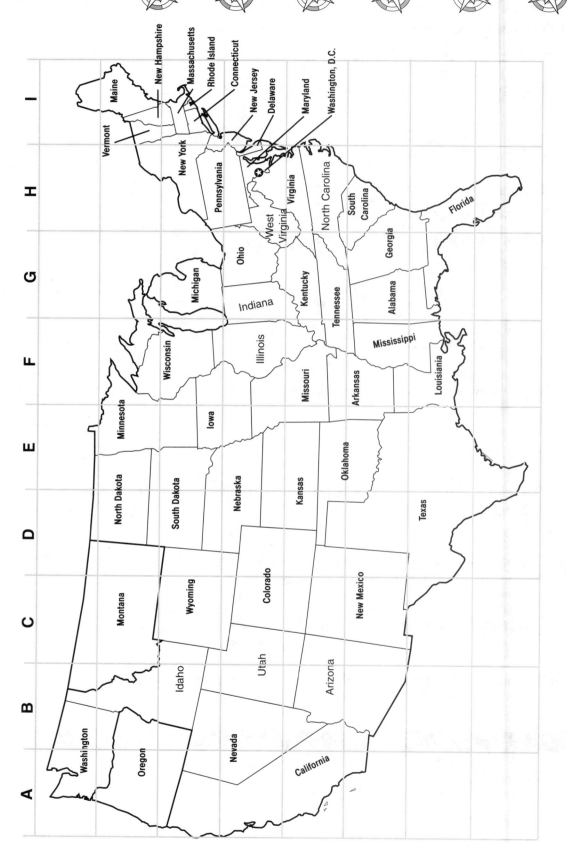

Most maps have grids placed on them to help you locate places. This is a map of the United States. You can see the lines going across the map vertically and horizontally. You can also see that there are numbers across the bottom and letters along the side. If you follow the line from the number 1 and stop where it meets the line at letter A, you will find the state of Washington. Use the grid to answer the questions on page 23.

Using a Grid (cont.)

Use the map and grid on page 22 to answer the questions below.

1. What three states are located entirely at 3I? _____

2. What state is located at 2C? _____

3. What state is located almost completely at 3G? _____

4. What state is almost completely located at 4H? _____

5. In which two coordinates would you find the state of Mississippi? _____

6. In which two coordinates would you find the state of Maine? _____

7. In which two coordinates would you find the state of Wisconsin? _____

8. What are four coordinates that are in Oregon? _____

9. What are three coordinates that are in Florida? _____

10. Find the state at 6C. What state is north of that one? _____

11. Find the state at 3G. What two states are south of that one? _____

12. What state is located at 7D? _____

Using Map Grids

Notice the grid on this world map. Use the map and grid to answer the questions on page 25.

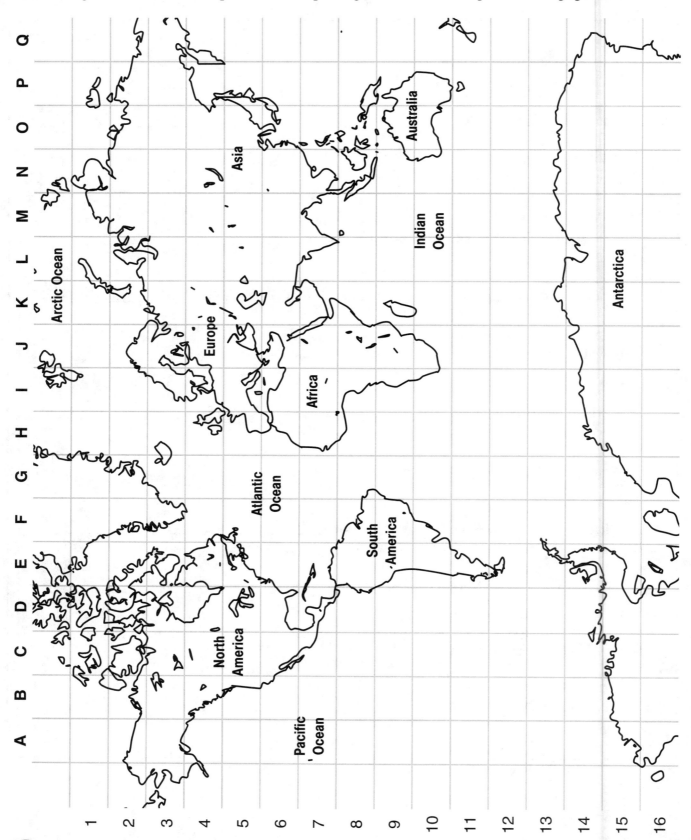

Using Map Grids *(cont.)*

1. What continent is located at 4L? _____

2. What continent is located at 10F? _____

3. If you were at 5C, would you be traveling in a car or in a boat? _____

4. What ocean is located at 8A? _____

5. What continent would you find at 9J? _____

6. What ocean would you find at 11M? _____

7. What continent is located at 3O? _____

8. What continent is located at 10P? _____

9. If you were at 8Q, would you be traveling in a car or in a boat? _____

10. What ocean is located at 1K? _____

11. What continent would you find at 16N? _____

12. What ocean would you find at 6G? _____

Globes

The earth is round, not flat. Even though flat maps can show different parts of our planet, a globe gives us a truer picture of what the Earth is really like. A globe is a model of the Earth. It is round like the Earth is round. A globe can rotate like the Earth rotates.

Color the water blue and the land green. Then answer the questions below.

1. What continents can be seen fully on the globe below?

   _____

   _____

2. What would you need to do in order to see Asia, Europe, and Africa?

   _____

   _____

3. Which is more like the Earth, a flat map or a globe?

   _____

   _____

   Why? _____

   _____

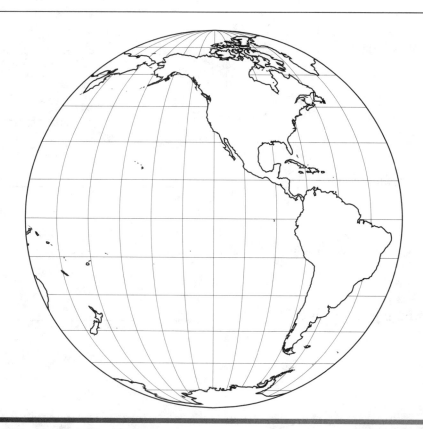

Latitude and Longitude

Like a grid, the lines of latitude and longitude help to locate places on the Earth. If a ship was having trouble at sea, the captain could radio for help and give the latitude and longitude of the ship's location. Using these lines, another plane or ship could come to the rescue.

There are two sets of lines that circle the globe. Lines of latitude run horizontally from east to west. The center line is the equator. Lines of longitude run vertically from north to south. The center line is the prime meridian. These lines are numbered in degrees. For example, a location on the globe might be at 30 degrees north latitude and 120 degrees east longitude.

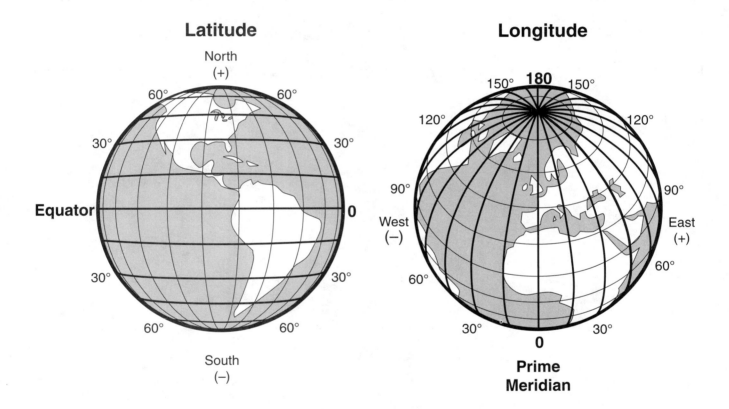

Answer the questions.

1. What are the lines that run from east to west? _____

2. What are the lines that run from north to south? _____

3. For what are the lines of latitude and longitude used? _____

4. What is the center line of latitude? _____

5. What is the center line of longitude? _____

Continents and Oceans

Before you learn more about the Earth or the globe, let's review the names of the continents and oceans. This world map shows the four oceans and seven continents. Use the world map below to answer the questions.

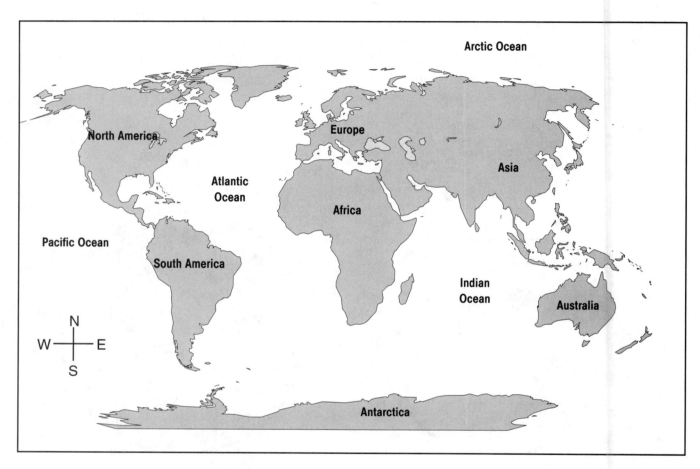

1. What is the name of the continent where you live? _____

2. Which two oceans border South America? _____

3. What ocean is north of Europe? _____

4. Which ocean is east of Africa? _____

5. Which ocean separates North America from Europe? _____

6. Which continent is closest to Antarctica? _____

Hemispheres

The Earth is divided into parts called hemispheres. Hemi means half. Sphere means ball or globe. A hemisphere is half of a globe. An imaginary line called the equator divides the globe into two parts. The part of the Earth that is above the equator is called the Northern Hemisphere. The part that is below the equator is called the Southern Hemisphere.

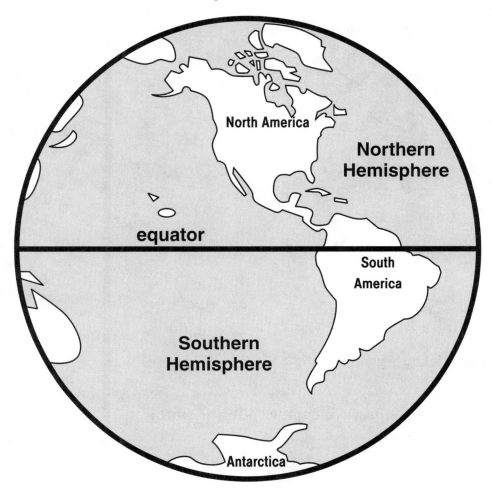

1. What does the word hemisphere mean? _____

2. What is the name of the imaginary line that divides the two hemispheres?_____

3. Trace the equator using a red crayon.

4. Draw a star on the Northern Hemisphere.

5. Draw a check mark on the Southern Hemisphere.

6. What two continents shown on this map are in the Southern Hemisphere?_____

7. In what hemisphere is North America located?_____

8. What continent does the equator pass through on this map? _____

More About Hemispheres

The Earth is divided into Northern and Southern Hemispheres. It is also divided in a way that separates the east from the west. An imaginary line called the prime meridian divides these two hemispheres. These hemispheres are called the Eastern and Western Hemispheres. Use the two halves of a globe below to answer the questions.

Western Hemisphere   **Eastern Hemisphere**

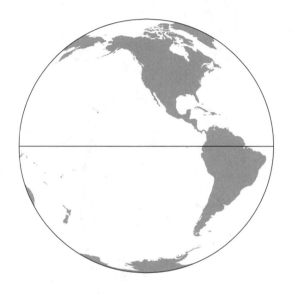   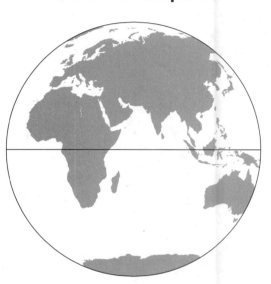

1. Europe is in which two hemispheres?

_____

2. South America is in how many hemispheres? Which ones?

_____

3. Which two continents lie completely in the southern hemisphere?

_____

4. In which two hemispheres do you live?

_____

5. What are all of the continents in the Southern Hemisphere?

_____

6. Which continent is completely in the Northern and Western Hemispheres?

_____

7. Which three oceans are in the Western Hemisphere?

_____

8. How many oceans are in the Eastern Hemisphere?

_____

Relief Maps

A relief map shows the geology of an area. This means that it shows landmarks, such as mountains, rivers, forests, valleys, and canyons. A relief map also tells the elevation of an area. The elevation tells how far above sea level an area is.

Below is a relief map of eastern Canada. The key shows lakes and also the elevation of the land.

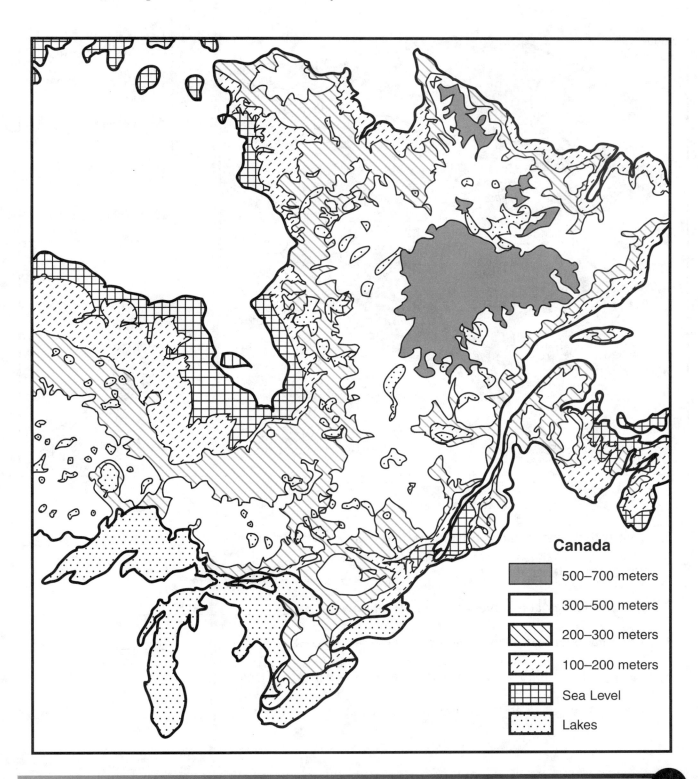

Canada

- 500–700 meters
- 300–500 meters
- 200–300 meters
- 100–200 meters
- Sea Level
- Lakes

Relief Maps *(cont.)*

This relief map of Alaska has been labeled to assist with answering the questions. Use the map to answer the questions below.

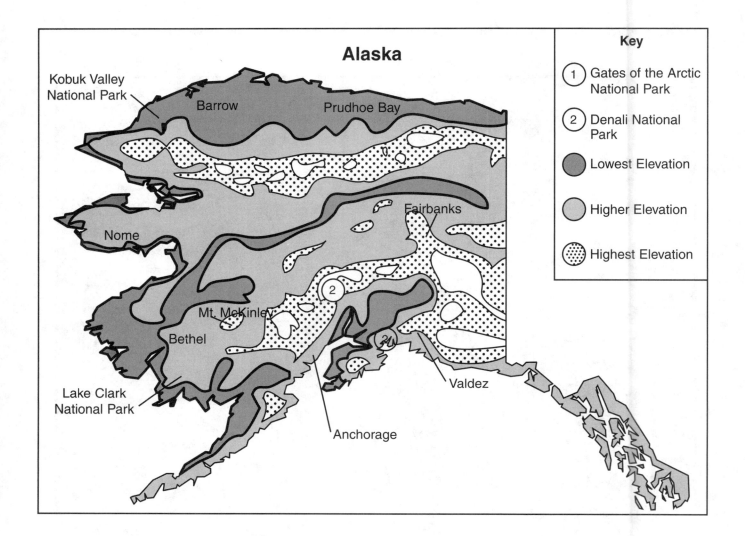

1. What is the name of the national park that is in a lower elevation? _____

2. Which city is located in a high elevation? _____

3. Is Mt. McKinley at a higher or lower elevation? _____

4. Which national park is in the southwestern part of Alaska? _____

5. Which park has higher areas of elevation, Kobuk Valley or Denali? _____

6. What do you notice about the elevation of areas near the ocean? _____

Population Maps

A population map provides information about the number of people who live in a certain area. A population map often has a key that is used much like a scale. Instead of measuring distance, this scale measures the number of people. For the map of the imaginary state below, one X equals two hundred people. Use the map to answer the questions.

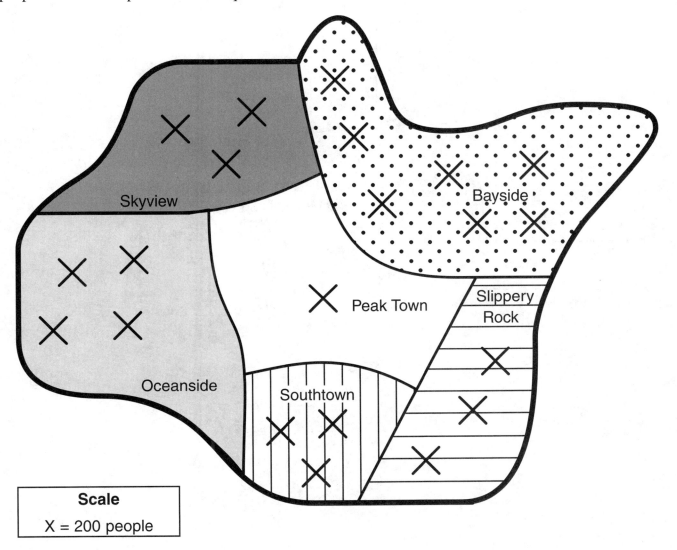

Scale

X = 200 people

1. How many people live in Bayside? _____

2. How many people live in Southtown? _____

3. Do more people live in Oceanside or in Skyview? _____

4. How many more people live in Bayside than Peak Town? _____

5. How many people live in this state? _____

6. How many people live in Skyview and Southtown combined? _____

Product Maps

Some maps are used to show the kinds of things that are grown, raised, or made in a certain place. For example, a map could show that a place is known for drilling oil or raising pigs. This kind of map is called a product map. Look at the product map below for the state of Texas. You can see that there are many products that are grown and raised there. Use the map to answer the questions below.

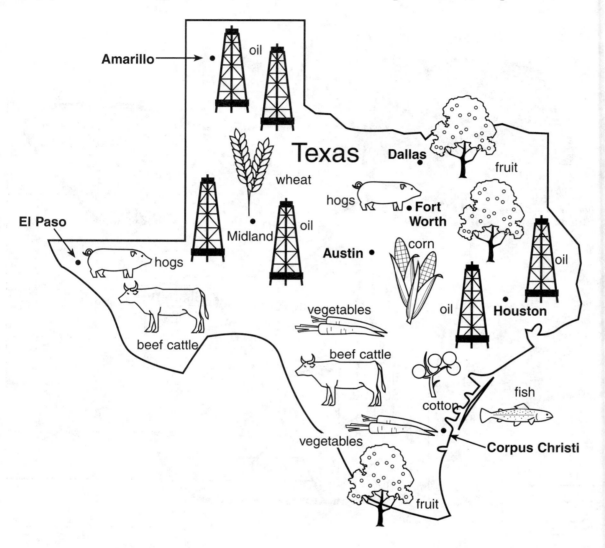

1. What kinds of foods are grown in Texas? _____

2. What is drilled from the ground in Texas? _____

3. What kinds of animals are raised in Texas? _____

4. What is the main product in the northern part of the state? _____

5. What two products are produced near Dallas? _____

6. What product comes from the water near Corpus Christi? _____

Create a Product Map

Create your own imaginary state. Draw a symbol to represent each product listed in the key. You can even create more additional products. Remember that products can also include things that are taken from the Earth, such as oil, minerals, or trees. Products can also include things that are made, such as clothes. Use your imagination and draw the products on the map of your state.

Name of State: _____

	Key
	fruit
	vegetables
	cotton
	cattle
	dairy
	fish

Weather Maps

There are many different kinds of weather maps. Some weather maps show high or low temperatures. Some show where it is snowing, raining, or where the sun is shining. Some weather maps even show the places where pollen is affecting people with allergies!

Use the weather map below to answer the questions about weather in Canada.

1. In which provinces is it sunny? _____

2. In which provinces is it snowy? _____

3. What two kinds of weather are in British Columbia? _____

4. What is another province that is having two kinds of weather? _____

5. What is the weather like in Saskatchewan? _____

6. What is the weather like in the northern part of Quebec? _____

Weather Maps *(cont.)*

Sometimes you will see extended forecasts for weather. These are predictions telling what the temperatures and weather conditions might be like. An extended forecast can also tell the percentage for chance of rain or snow. The extended forecast below is for Phoenix, Arizona, in July.

Date	Weather		High/Low Temperatures	Chance of Precipitation
July 13		Partly Cloudy	110°/87°	30°
July 14		Partly Cloudy	107°/88°	0%
July 15		Mostly Cloudy	111°/95°	10%
July 16		Isolated Thunderstorms	107°/83°	30%
July 17		Isolated Thunderstorms	104°/85°	40%
July 18		Partly Cloudy	109°/86°	20%
July 19		Partly Cloudy	112°/87°	0%
July 20		Partly Cloudy	111°/86°	0%

1. What is the forecasted low temperature for July 15? _____

2. What is the forecasted high temperature for July 18?_____

3. Which days have rain in the forecast?_____

4. What is the chance of rain for July 15?_____

5. Which day will likely be the hottest? _____

Weather Maps *(cont.)*

The map below is of the Western United States. This map shows severe weather conditions, hazardous weather, severe thunderstorms, and extreme heat. Use the map and key to answer the questions.

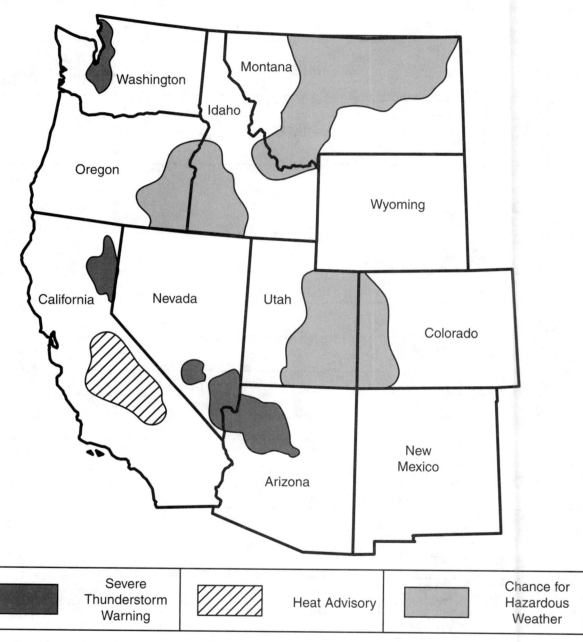

Key		Severe Thunderstorm Warning		Heat Advisory		Chance for Hazardous Weather

1. Which states have thunderstorm warnings? _____

2. Which states have the chance for hazardous weather? _____

3. Which state has a chance for the most hazardous weather? _____

4. Which states will not have any strong weather or extreme heat? _____

5. Which state has a heat advisory? _____

6. Which part of Nevada will experience the most severe thunderstorms? _____

Practice Test 1

Use the compass rose and key to answer the questions.

  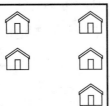

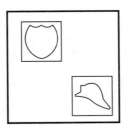

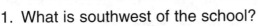

Key	
	house
	school
	park
	picnic area
	police station
	fire station
	bank
	pizza parlor
	hospital
	airport

1. What is southwest of the school?

   (A) picnic area   (C) park

   (B) bank   (D) police station

2. If you were at the hospital, what direction would you go to get to the fire station?

   (A) southwest   (C) southeast

   (B) northwest   (D) northeast

3. What is in the northeast part of the map?

   (A) houses   (C) a school

   (B) a pizza parlor   (D) an airport

4. What is in the southeast part of the map?

   (A) houses   (C) a bank

   (B) a hospital   (D) a park

5. If you are at the pizza parlor and wanted to take a car to get to the airport, which three directions would you need to drive in order to get there?

   (A) south, north, west

   (B) south, east, north

   (C) north, west, south

   (D) south, west, north

6. Which two buildings are side by side?

   (A) the school and the airport

   (B) the fire station and the police station

   (C) the bank and the pizza parlor

   (D) the school and the fire station

Practice Test 2

Use the scale to answer the questions about the map.

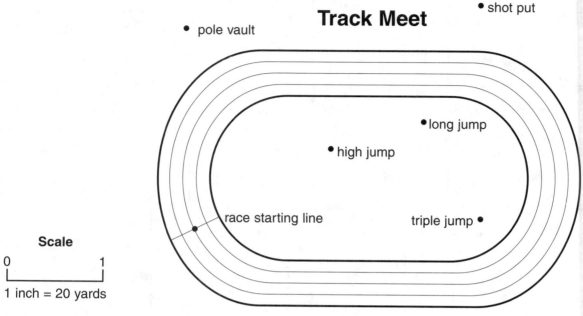

Track Meet

• shot put

• pole vault

• long jump

• high jump

race starting line

triple jump •

Scale

0 ————————— 1

1 inch = 20 yards

1. On the map, two inches equals
   - (A) 20 yards
   - (B) 1 yard
   - (C) 40 yards
   - (D) 2 yards

2. How many yards is the race starting line from the triple jump area? (Choose the closest answer.)
   - (A) 40 yards
   - (B) 60 yards
   - (C) 4 yards
   - (D) 80 yards

3. How far is the pole vault area from the high jump? (Choose the closest answer.)
   - (A) 3 yards
   - (B) 60 yards
   - (C) 40 yards
   - (D) 70 yards

4. About how far is the race starting line from the shot put? (Choose the closest answer.)
   - (A) about 110 yards
   - (B) about 5 1/2 yards
   - (C) about 80 yards
   - (D) about 120 yards

5. How far would you walk if you went from the high jump area to the triple jump and then to the shot put? (Choose the closest answer.)
   - (A) 40 yards
   - (B) 12 yards
   - (C) 100 yards
   - (D) 80 yards

6. How far would it be to walk from the pole vault to the race starting line and then to the high jump? (Choose the closest answer.)
   - (A) 5 yards
   - (B) 75 yards
   - (C) 90 yards
   - (D) 60 yards

Practice Test 3

Use the mileage chart to answer each question.

	Houston, TX	Portland, OR	St. Louis, MO	Wichita, KS
Austin, TX	186	2069	823	548
Madison, WI	1137	1950	358	676
Salt Lake City, UT	1483	767	1337	1003
Omaha, NE	865	1654	449	298

1. How far apart are Austin and Houston?
   - (A) 2,069
   - (B) 186
   - (C) 767
   - (D) 449

2. How many miles apart are Salt Lake City and Portland?
   - (A) 767
   - (B) 1,483
   - (C) 1,950
   - (D) 358

3. Which city on the chart is closest to Madison?
   - (A) Wichita
   - (B) Houston
   - (C) St. Louis
   - (D) Austin

4. Which city on the chart is farthest away from Omaha?
   - (A) Portland
   - (B) Houston
   - (C) St. Louis
   - (D) Wichita

5. Which city on the chart is closest to Salt Lake City?
   - (A) Wichita
   - (B) Houston
   - (C) St. Louis
   - (D) Portland

6. If you were in Salt Lake City, how many miles farther is it to go to St. Louis than Portland?
   - (A) 344
   - (B) 570
   - (C) 550
   - (D) 1,275

Practice Test 4

Use the map and grid to answer the questions below.

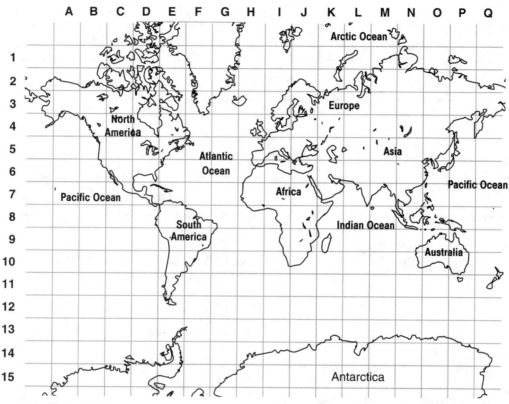

1. What is located at G7?
   - Ⓐ the Atlantic Ocean
   - Ⓑ North America
   - Ⓒ the Pacific Ocean
   - Ⓓ Africa

2. What continent is located at E8?
   - Ⓐ the Pacific Ocean
   - Ⓑ South America
   - Ⓒ Asia
   - Ⓓ the Indian Ocean

3. M6 and P3 are both a part of what?
   - Ⓐ North America
   - Ⓑ the Atlantic Ocean
   - Ⓒ Europe
   - Ⓓ Asia

4. What ocean is north of K3?
   - Ⓐ the Indian Ocean
   - Ⓑ the Arctic Ocean
   - Ⓒ the Atlantic Ocean
   - Ⓓ both the Atlantic and Pacific Oceans

5. Which of the coordinates below is on land?
   - Ⓐ P3
   - Ⓑ L8
   - Ⓒ H2
   - Ⓓ J11

6. Which of the coordinates below is not in the ocean?
   - Ⓐ A13
   - Ⓑ G14
   - Ⓒ C5
   - Ⓓ L12

Practice Test 5

Answer the questions about the latitude, longitude, and hemispheres.

1. What is the invisible line that runs from east to west?
   - (A) prime meridian
   - (B) Western Hemisphere
   - (C) Eastern Hemisphere
   - (D) equator

2. What is the invisible line that runs from north to south?
   - (A) prime meridian
   - (B) equator
   - (C) the Northern Hemisphere
   - (D) the Southern Hemisphere

3. The lines that run from east to west are lines of
   - (A) the prime meridian
   - (B) longitude
   - (C) latitude
   - (D) none of the above

4. Australia is in which hemisphere?
   - (A) Northern
   - (B) Southern
   - (C) Eastern
   - (D) both Southern and Eastern

5. Europe is in which two hemispheres?
   - (A) Northern and Western
   - (B) Northern and Eastern
   - (C) Southern and Western
   - (D) Southern and Eastern

6. In which two hemispheres is North America located?
   - (A) Northern and Western
   - (B) Northern and Eastern
   - (C) Southern and Western
   - (D) Southern and Eastern

Practice Test 6

Answer the questions below.

1. What kind of map tells about where corn is grown?
   - (A) world map
   - (B) weather map
   - (C) product map
   - (D) population map

2. What kind of map tells how many people live in a place where it rains a lot?
   - (A) country map
   - (B) product map
   - (C) population map
   - (D) city map

3. What kind of map would you use to find out where it is raining?
   - (A) product map
   - (B) world map
   - (C) weather map
   - (D) temperature map

4. Hurricanes would be shown on what kind of map?
   - (A) world map
   - (B) weather map
   - (C) ocean map
   - (D) product map

5. A product map might show
   - (A) the kinds of crops that are grown in a certain place.
   - (B) where oil is drilled.
   - (C) people earn a living by fishing.
   - (D) all of the above.

6. What kind of map would you use to find out if growing fruit would be affected by a drought?
   - (A) product map
   - (B) population map
   - (C) weather map
   - (D) state map

Answer Sheet

Test Practice 1	Test Practice 2	Test Practice 3
1. Ⓐ Ⓑ Ⓒ Ⓓ	1. Ⓐ Ⓑ Ⓒ Ⓓ	1. Ⓐ Ⓑ Ⓒ Ⓓ
2. Ⓐ Ⓑ Ⓒ Ⓓ	2. Ⓐ Ⓑ Ⓒ Ⓓ	2. Ⓐ Ⓑ Ⓒ Ⓓ
3. Ⓐ Ⓑ Ⓒ Ⓓ	3. Ⓐ Ⓑ Ⓒ Ⓓ	3. Ⓐ Ⓑ Ⓒ Ⓓ
4. Ⓐ Ⓑ Ⓒ Ⓓ	4. Ⓐ Ⓑ Ⓒ Ⓓ	4. Ⓐ Ⓑ Ⓒ Ⓓ
5. Ⓐ Ⓑ Ⓒ Ⓓ	5. Ⓐ Ⓑ Ⓒ Ⓓ	5. Ⓐ Ⓑ Ⓒ Ⓓ
6. Ⓐ Ⓑ Ⓒ Ⓓ	6. Ⓐ Ⓑ Ⓒ Ⓓ	6. Ⓐ Ⓑ Ⓒ Ⓓ

Test Practice 4	Test Practice 5	Test Practice 6
1. Ⓐ Ⓑ Ⓒ Ⓓ	1. Ⓐ Ⓑ Ⓒ Ⓓ	1. Ⓐ Ⓑ Ⓒ Ⓓ
2. Ⓐ Ⓑ Ⓒ Ⓓ	2. Ⓐ Ⓑ Ⓒ Ⓓ	2. Ⓐ Ⓑ Ⓒ Ⓓ
3. Ⓐ Ⓑ Ⓒ Ⓓ	3. Ⓐ Ⓑ Ⓒ Ⓓ	3. Ⓐ Ⓑ Ⓒ Ⓓ
4. Ⓐ Ⓑ Ⓒ Ⓓ	4. Ⓐ Ⓑ Ⓒ Ⓓ	4. Ⓐ Ⓑ Ⓒ Ⓓ
5. Ⓐ Ⓑ Ⓒ Ⓓ	5. Ⓐ Ⓑ Ⓒ Ⓓ	5. Ⓐ Ⓑ Ⓒ Ⓓ
6. Ⓐ Ⓑ Ⓒ Ⓓ	6. Ⓐ Ⓑ Ⓒ Ⓓ	6. Ⓐ Ⓑ Ⓒ Ⓓ

Answer Key

Page 4

1. a place
2. any three of the following: world, country, state, city, weather, product, population
3. any two of the following: streets, highways, schools, attractions, landmarks
4. high and low temperatures, current weather conditions, where people are affected by allergies
5. the places where certain products are produced
6. the number of people who live in a certain place
7. It is round and turns.
8. the Earth

Page 5

1. South
2. North
3. West
4. SW
5. NE
6. NW

Page 7

1. Highway C
2. Highway D
3. southwest
4. northeast
5. southeast
6. Highway A
7. Highway D
8. the airport
9. the zoo
10. west

Page 8

1. Mountain Road
2. Green Street
3. the dog park
4. the soccer field
5. east and south
6. National Forest

Page 9

1. symbol
2. picture
3. symbol
4. symbol
5. symbol
6. picture
7. picture
8. symbol
9. symbol
10. symbol
11. picture
12. picture

Page 11

1. one
2. train track
3. southeast
4. four
5. two
6. three
7. southwest
8. by train
9. Riverside
10. one

Page 12

1. Lake Placid, Glen Falls
2. Catskill Mountains
3. a river
4. Buffalo
5. Lake Ontario, Lake Erie
6. Albany
7. mountains
8. a river

Page 13

1. England
2. Ireland
3. Cardiff
4. north
5. northern
6. a river
7. Cambrian Mountains
8. Dee

Page 16

1. 1 mile
2. 5 inches
3. 5 miles
4. 3 ½ centimeters
5. 3 ½ kilometers
6. 3 ½ miles
7. 4 ½ kilometers
8. 2 ½ miles

Answer Key (cont.)

Page 17

1. 30 yards
2. 2 inches, 20 yards
3. 45 yards
4. 35 yards
5. 65 yards
6. 85 yards

Page 19

1. 6 km
2. 22.5 km
3. Palace of Fine Arts
4. 13.5 km
5. 9 km
6. 39 km
7. It is farther to go from the airport to the zoo.
8. 46.5 km
9. 24 km
10. 28.5 km

Page 21

1. 1,452
2. 1,507
3. Amarillo
4. Dallas
5. 1,319
6. 2,325
7. almost 27 hours
8. a little more than 33 hours
9. Chicago
10. Minneapolis

Page 23

1. Massachusetts, Rhode Island, and Connecticut
2. Montana
3. Michigan
4. Maryland
5. 6F, 7F
6. 1I, 2I

7. 2F, 3F
8. 2A, 3A, 2B, 3B
9. 7G, 7H, 8H
10. Colorado
11. Indiana and Ohio
12. Texas

Page 25

1. Europe
2. South America
3. car
4. the Pacific Ocean
5. Africa
6. the Indian Ocean
7. Asia
8. Australia
9. boat
10. the Arctic Ocean
11. Antarctica
12. the Atlantic Ocean

Page 26

1. North America and South America
2. You would need to turn the globe around.
3. A globe is more like the Earth because it is round and it turns.

Page 27

1. lines of latitude
2. lines of longitude
3. They are used for locating places on the globe/Earth.
4. the equator
5. the prime meridian

Page 28

1. answers will vary
2. the Atlantic and the Pacific Oceans
3. the Arctic Ocean
4. the Indian Ocean
5. the Atlantic Ocean
6. South America

Answer Key (cont.)

Page 29
1. Hemisphere means half of a ball or globe.
2. the equator
3. 3–5. Answers will vary.
6. South America and Antarctica
7. the Northern Hemisphere
8. South America

Page 30
1. Northern and Eastern
2. three (Northern, Southern, and Western)
3. Antarctica and Australia
4. Answers will vary.
5. South America, Africa, Antarctica, Australia
6. North America
7. Atlantic Ocean, Pacific Ocean, Arctic Ocean
8. four

Page 32
1. Kobuk Valley National Park
2. Fairbanks
3. higher
4. Lake Clark National Park
5. Denali National Park
6. Areas near the ocean are at lower elevations.

Page 33
1. 1,400
2. 600
3. Oceanside
4. 1,200
5. 4,200
6. 1,200

Page 34
1. fruit, vegetables, corn, wheat
2. oil
3. hogs, beef cattle
4. oil
5. fruit and hogs
6. fish

Page 36
1. Saskatchewan and Ontario
2. Yukon Territory and Nunavut
3. rainy and cloudy
4. Quebec
5. sunny
6. cloudy

Page 37
1. 95°
2. 109°
3. July 16 and July 17
4. 10%
5. July 19

Page 38
1. California, Nevada, Washington, and Arizona
2. Montana, Oregon, Idaho, Utah, and Colorado
3. Montana
4. Wyoming and New Mexico
5. California
6. the Southeastern part

Page 39
1. C	3. D	5. B
2. A	4. A	6. C

Page 40
1. C	3. C	5. D
2. B	4. C	6. B

Page 41
1. B	3. C	5. D
2. A	4. A	6. B

Page 42
1. A	3. D	5. A
2. B	4. B	6. C

Page 43
1. D	3. C	5. B
2. A	4. D	6. A

Page 44
1. C	3. C	5. D
2. C	4. B	6. C